student
cookbook

THE AUSTRALIAN
Women's Weekly

contents

Learning to cook has never been so easy with this book as your go-to-guide. All the recipes use basic fresh ingredients that can be purchased inexpensively from your local shops. Throw on your apron and get started – you'll be surprised how quickly your confidence grows.

Pamela Clark

Editorial & food director

Australian cup and spoon measurements are metric. A conversion chart appears on page 77.

simple salads

Salads are a great way to incorporate vegetables into your diet.
Literally thrown together, they allow you to be creative and use
up what's in the fridge. Here are some ideas to get you started.

greek salad

- ¼ cup (60ml) olive oil
- 1 tablespoon lemon juice
- 1 tablespoon white wine vinegar
- 1 tablespoon finely chopped fresh oregano
- 1 clove garlic, crushed
- 3 medium tomatoes (450g), cut into wedges
- 2 lebanese cucumbers (260g), chopped coarsely
- 200g (6½ ounces) fetta, chopped coarsely
- 1 small red onion (100g), sliced thinly
- 1 small red capsicum (bell pepper) (150g), sliced thinly
- ½ cup (75g) seeded black olives

1 Whisk oil, juice, vinegar, oregano and garlic in a large bowl.

2 Add all ingredients to bowl; toss gently to combine. Season to taste.

serving suggestion Serve with beef or lamb kebabs.

tips For an authentic, Greek way of serving this salad, leave the fetta in a whole piece and sit it on top of the salad. Anchovies can be added to impart a salty flavour.

prep time 20 minutes
serves 4
**nutritional count per
serving** 25.8g total fat
(9.6g saturated fat); 1359kJ
(325 cal); 10.8g carbohydrate;
11.5g protein; 3.2g fibre

prep + cook time
20 minutes **serves** 4
**nutritional count per
serving** 16.9g total fat
(3.7g saturated fat);
1522kJ (364 cal);
19.5g carbohydrate;
30.9g protein; 5.2g fibre

salad niçoise

- 200g (6½ ounces) baby green beans, trimmed
- 2 tablespoons olive oil
- 1 tablespoon lemon juice
- 2 tablespoons white wine vinegar
- 4 medium tomatoes (600g), cut into wedges
- 4 hard-boiled eggs (see tip), quartered
- 425g (13½ ounces) canned tuna in springwater, drained, flaked
- ½ cup (80g) drained caperberries, rinsed
- ½ cup (60g) seeded small black olives
- ¼ cup firmly packed fresh flat-leaf parsley leaves
- 440g (14 ounces) canned whole baby new potatoes, rinsed, drained, halved

1 Boil, steam or microwave beans until just tender; drain. Rinse under cold water; drain.

2 Whisk oil, juice and vinegar in a large bowl, add beans and remaining salad ingredients; toss gently to combine.

serving suggestion
Salad niçoise is traditionally served on its own as a light meal, accompanied by warm crusty bread and a glass of light red wine. As a main course, serve salad with barbecued fish or other grilled seafood, in place of the canned tuna.

tip To hard-boil eggs, cover room temperature eggs with cold water in a small saucepan. Cover; bring to the boil; remove lid. Boil eggs, uncovered, 5 minutes. Remove pan from heat and drain eggs carefully. Place cooked eggs in a bowl of cold water. Tap eggs against the side of the bowl to crack shells; peel gently.

chicken caesar salad

- 4 slices white bread (180g)
- 2 tablespoons olive oil
- 4 rashers rindless bacon (260g), sliced thinly
- 3 cups (480g) coarsely chopped barbecued chicken
- 1 large cos (romaine) lettuce, trimmed, torn
- 6 green onions (scallions), sliced thinly
- 1 cup (80g) shaved parmesan

caesar dressing

- ¾ cup (225g) whole-egg mayonnaise
- 1 tablespoon lemon juice
- 4 drained anchovy fillets, chopped finely
- 3 teaspoons dijon mustard
- 1 tablespoon water

1 Preheat oven to 180°C/350°F.

2 Make caesar dressing.

3 Remove crusts from bread; discard crusts, cut bread into 2cm (¾-inch) squares; toss with oil in a medium bowl. Place bread on an oven tray in a single layer; toast in oven 10 minutes.

4 Cook bacon in a small frying pan, over medium heat, stirring, 5 minutes until browned and crisp. Drain on paper towel.

5 Place half the chicken, half the bacon, half the croûtons and half the dressing in a large bowl with lettuce, add half the onion and half the parmesan; toss gently to combine.

6 Divide salad between serving plates. Top with remaining chicken, bacon, croûtons, onion and parmesan; drizzle with remaining dressing. Season to taste.

caesar dressing Blend or process ingredients until smooth.

prep + cook time 25 minutes
serves 4
**nutritional count per
serving** 49.9g total fat
(12.3g saturated fat); 3390kJ
(811 cal); 35.6g carbohydrate;
52.6g protein; 6.3g fibre

tips Pasta salad is one of those favourites that has as many variations as there are cooks who make it. Because it's eaten cold, it's ideal for picnics or lunchboxes.

pasta salad

- 250g (8 ounces) orecchiette pasta
- 2 tablespoons drained sun-dried tomatoes, chopped coarsely
- 1 small red onion (100g), sliced thinly
- 1 small green capsicum (bell pepper) (150g), sliced thinly
- ½ cup coarsely chopped fresh flat-leaf parsley

sun-dried tomato dressing

- 1 tablespoon sun-dried tomato pesto
- 1 tablespoon white wine vinegar
- 2 tablespoons olive oil

1 Cook pasta in a large saucepan of boiling water until just tender; drain. Rinse under cold water; drain.

2 Make sun-dried tomato dressing.

3 Place pasta in a large bowl with salad ingredients and dressing; toss gently to combine. Season to taste.

sun-dried tomato dressing Place ingredients in a screw-top jar; shake well.

serving suggestion Serve with grilled lamb chops or chicken.

prep + cook time 25 minutes
serves 4
nutritional count per serving 12g total fat (1.9g saturated fat); 1405kJ (336 cal); 46g carbohydrate; 8.8g protein; 3.6g fibre

tip Tabbouleh is traditionally made with a great deal of chopped fresh flat-leaf parsley and varying smaller amounts of burghul, green onion and mint. Go easy on the burghul: too much and the completed tabbouleh will be heavy instead of fluffy and light, as it is meant to be.

tabbouleh

- ¼ cup (40g) burghul
- 3 medium tomatoes (450g)
- 3 cups coarsely chopped fresh flat-leaf parsley
- 3 green onions (scallions), chopped finely
- ¼ cup coarsely chopped fresh mint
- ¼ cup (60ml) lemon juice
- ¼ cup (60ml) olive oil

1 Place burghul in a medium shallow bowl. Halve tomatoes, scoop pulp from tomato over burghul. Chop tomato flesh finely; spread over burghul. Cover; refrigerate 1 hour.

2 Combine burghul mixture in a large bowl with remaining ingredients. Season to taste.

serving suggestions
Tabbouleh is ideal served with Middle Eastern meals. Serve it with garlic chicken, beef or lamb kebabs. For an easy lunch enclose tabbouleh with rare roast beef in Lebanese bread.

prep time 30 minutes
(+ refrigeration) **serves** 4
**nutritional count per
serving** 14.1g total fat
(2g saturated fat); 790kJ
(189 cal); 9.2g carbohydrate;
3.4g protein; 5.6g fibre

tip Pancetta can be replaced with thin strips of bacon.

warm balsamic mushroom salad

- **8 slices pancetta (120g)**
- **½ cup (125ml) balsamic italian dressing**
- **⅓ cup (80ml) water**
- **500g (1 pound) small button mushrooms**
- **1 teaspoon fresh thyme leaves**
- **90g (3 ounces) mixed salad leaves**
- **90g (3 ounces) fetta, crumbled**

prep + cook time 10 minutes **serves** 4 **nutritional count per serving** 19.9g total fat (6g saturated fat); 1066kJ (255 cal); 3.1g carbohydrate; 14.6g protein; 3.8g fibre

1 Cook pancetta in a heated oiled large frying pan, over medium heat, 3 minutes or until crisp. When cool enough to handle, break into large pieces.

2 Heat dressing and the water in same frying pan; cook mushrooms and thyme, stirring, until mushrooms are tender and liquid has almost evaporated. Season to taste.

3 Combine mushrooms, salad leaves and pancetta in a large bowl; toss gently. Serve topped with fetta.

serving suggestion
Serve salad as a main meal with grilled chicken, beef, lamb or fish. It can also be eaten cold, so it's ideal for lunchboxes and picnics.

asian crispy noodle salad

- ½ medium wombok
  (napa cabbage) (500g),
  shredded finely
- 230g (7 ounces) canned
  water chestnuts, drained,
  sliced thinly
- 150g (4½ ounces) snow
  peas, trimmed, sliced thinly
- 1 large red capsicum
  (bell pepper) (350g),
  sliced thinly
- 100g (3 ounces) packet
  fried noodles
- ½ cup (50g) roasted
  unsalted cashews,
  chopped coarsely
- 1 cup loosely packed fresh
  coriander (cilantro) leaves

sesame soy dressing

- 1 teaspoon sesame oil
- ¼ cup (60ml) soy sauce
- 1 tablespoon sweet
  chilli sauce
- 2 tablespoons lime juice

1 Make sesame
soy dressing.
2 Place wombok, water
chestnuts, snow peas,
capsicum and fried
noodles in a medium
bowl; toss to combine.
3 Divide salad between
serving bowls; sprinkle
with cashews and
coriander, drizzle with
dressing. Season to taste.

sesame soy dressing
Place ingredients in a
screw-top jar; shake well.
serving suggestion
Serve with Chinese
barbecued pork, stir-fried
beef or barbecued
hot dogs.

prep time 15 minutes
serves 4
**nutritional count per
serving** 10.8g fat
(2.2g saturated fat);
869kJ (208 cal);
19.1g carbohydrate;
8.3g protein; 6.4g fibre

tips For extra heat add 1 finely chopped chilli to the dressing. Add the noodles just before serving, to prevent them going soggy.

tips We used red-skinned potatoes in this recipe. Bacon can be fried a few hours ahead; cover, refrigerate.

german hot potato salad

- 500g (1 pound) potatoes, unpeeled, cut into 2cm (¾-inch) cubes
- 2 rindless bacon rashers (130g), sliced thinly
- 1 small red onion (100g), sliced thinly
- ½ teaspoon black mustard seeds
- ⅓ cup finely chopped fresh flat-leaf parsley

sweet dijon dressing
- 2 tablespoons cider vinegar
- 2 tablespoons olive oil
- 2 teaspoons dijon mustard
- ½ teaspoon caster (superfine) sugar

1 Boil, steam or microwave potato until tender; drain.

2 Meanwhile, make sweet dijon dressing.

3 Cook bacon in a heated medium frying pan, over medium heat, stirring, 5 minutes or until crisp; drain on paper towel. Cook onion in same pan, stirring, 5 minutes until softened. Add mustard seeds; cook, stirring, 1 minute.

4 Combine potato, bacon, onion mixture, parsley and dressing in a large bowl. Season to taste.

sweet dijon dressing Combine ingredients in a screw-top jar; shake well.

serving suggestion Serve with grilled pork chops.

prep + cook time 30 minutes serves 4 nutritional count per serving 13.7g total fat (3.1g saturated fat); 1012kJ (242 cal); 17g carbohydrate; 10g protein; 3.2g fibre

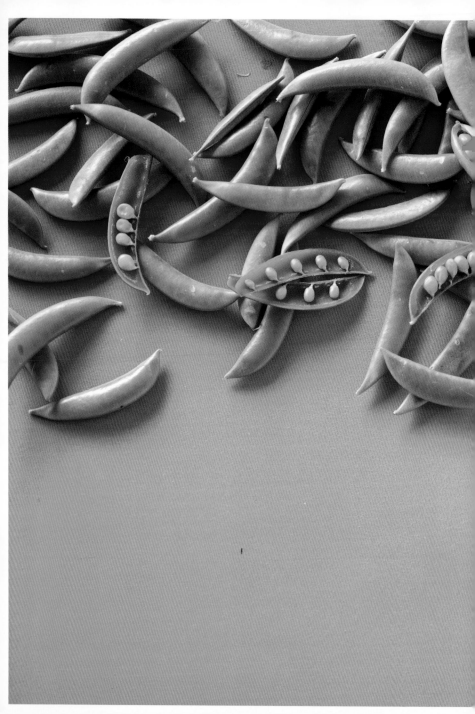

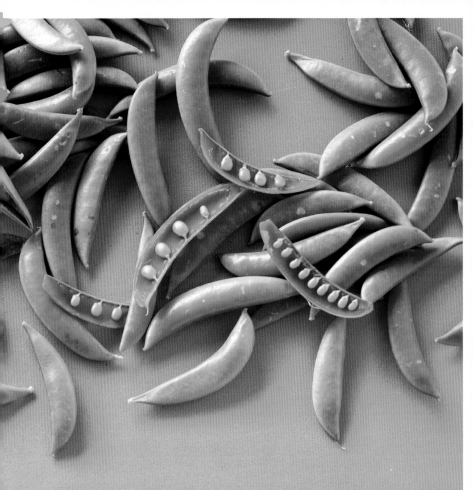

quick & easy meals

Long day at work? Uni assignment due? Don't stress. These fast dinners are for those days when you don't have time to fuss. Take a short break and unwind in the kitchen while you cook.

tomato & capsicum soup

- 800g (1½ pounds) canned peri-peri style diced tomatoes
- 1⅓ cups (285g) drained jarred char-grilled capsicum (bell pepper) in oil
- 3 cups (750ml) chicken stock
- 400g (12½ ounces) canned cannellini beans, rinsed, drained

1 Combine tomatoes, capsicum and half the stock in a large saucepan; bring to the boil. Reduce heat to low; simmer, covered, about 20 minutes; cool 10 minutes.

2 Using a hand-held mixer, process the soup in pan until smooth. Add remaining stock and beans; stir over medium heat until hot. Season to taste.

serving suggestions Serve with warm crusty bread or as an entrée to a simple roast dinner.

tips If you are unable to find peri-peri tomatoes, add some peri-peri sauce to taste. For a nice twist in summer, serve chilled or at room temperature, followed by a simple salad.

prep + cook time
30 minutes **serves** 4
**nutritional count per
serving** 7.7g total fat
(0.8g saturated fat);
1028kJ (246 cal);
31.3g carbohydrate;
12.4g protein; 9.7g fibre

prep + cook time
25 minutes **serves** 4
**nutritional count per
serving** 19.9g total fat
(7.6g saturated fat);
2643kJ (631 cal);
84.2g carbohydrate;
23.9g protein; 6.6g fibre

roasted eggplant & chorizo pizza

- 2 x 335g pizza bases
- 320g (10 ounces) jarred char-grilled eggplant in oil, drained, chopped coarsely
- ½ cup (75g) seeded kalamata olives
- 1 chorizo sausage (170g), sliced thinly
- ½ cup (50g) coarsely grated pizza cheese

1 Preheat oven to 220°C/425°F. Oil two oven trays.

2 Top pizza bases with eggplant, olives and chorizo, sprinkle with cheese. Cook, uncovered, about 15 minutes. Sprinkle pizzas with fresh oregano, if you like.

serving suggestion Serve with a green salad.

tip Chorizo sausage is a highly seasoned, coarsely-ground pork sausage flavoured with garlic, chilli powder and other spices. It's widely used in both Mexican and Spanish cookery. Mexican chorizo is made with fresh pork, while the Spanish version uses smoked pork.

pappardelle carbonara

- 8 slices prosciutto (120g), sliced thinly
- 375g (12 ounces) pappardelle pasta
- 3 eggs
- ½ cup (125ml) pouring cream
- ½ cup (40g) finely grated parmesan
- ¼ cup coarsely chopped fresh flat-leaf parsley

1 Cook prosciutto in a heated oiled large frying pan over medium-high heat, 3 minutes or until crisp; remove from pan.

2 Cook pasta in a large saucepan of boiling water until tender; drain, reserving ½ cup (125ml) cooking liquid. Return pasta to pan over low heat.

3 Meanwhile, lightly beat eggs, cream and parmesan in a large jug.

4 Add egg mixture, reserved cooking liquid, half the parsley and half the prosciutto to pasta. Toss gently, briefly over the heat; season to taste.

5 Serve pasta topped with remaining prosciutto and parsley.

serving suggestion
Serve with garlic bread and a leafy salad.

tips Pappardelle are flat, wide pasta ribbons, available dried or fresh. Tagliatelle or fettuccine can be substituted. Try using grated pecorino – romano or pepato – instead of parmesan.

prep + cook time
10 minutes **serves** 4
**nutritional count per
serving** 22.6g total fat
(12.7g saturated fat); 2349kJ
(562 cal); 65g carbohydrate;
22.7g protein; 3.3g fibre

tips Chicken and anything it is marinated in needs to be fully cooked to rid it of harmful bacteria. Wash any kitchen equipment that comes in contact with raw chicken thoroughly with warm soapy water. Chicken thighs are delicious, but are often overlooked in favour of breast fillets. The thigh is full of flavour and will not dry out as easily as the breast.

pesto chicken with grilled zucchini

- 6 medium zucchini (720g), sliced thickly lengthways
- olive oil cooking spray
- 1 teaspoon finely grated lemon rind
- ⅓ cup (90g) sun-dried tomato pesto
- 4 x 200g (6½ ounces) chicken thigh fillets, cut into thirds

1 Spray zucchini with oil; cook on a heated oiled grill plate (or barbecue or grill), in batches, 2 minutes each side or until tender. Place zucchini in a medium bowl; sprinkle with rind. Cover to keep warm.

2 Combine pesto and chicken in a large bowl. Cook chicken on a heated oiled grill plate (or grill or barbecue), brushing occasionally with pesto mixture, 4 minutes each side or until cooked through. Serve chicken with zucchini.

serving suggestion Serve with baby rocket leaves or a leafy green salad, if you like.

prep + cook time
25 minutes serves 4
nutritional count per
serving 35.1g total fat
(10.3g saturated fat);
2023kJ (484 cal);
4.3g carbohydrate;
36.7g protein; 2.8g fibre

ginger & teriyaki beef stir-fry

- 2 tablespoons teriyaki sauce
- 2 tablespoons hoisin sauce
- 1 tablespoon mirin
- ½ teaspoon peanut oil
- 200g (6½ ounces) beef fillet, sliced thinly
- 1 large red capsicum (bell pepper) (350g), sliced thinly
- 200g (6½ ounces) snow peas, trimmed, sliced lengthways
- 1 medium carrot (120g), cut into matchsticks
- 115g (3½ ounces) baby corn, quartered lengthways
- 4cm (1½-inch) piece fresh ginger (20g), sliced thinly
- 2 tablespoons water

1 Combine sauces and mirin in a small jug.
2 Heat oil in a wok; stir-fry beef over high heat about 4 minutes or until browned. Remove from wok.
3 Add capsicum, peas, carrot, corn, ginger and the water to wok; stir-fry until carrot is almost tender. Return beef to wok with sauce mixture; stir-fry until hot. Season to taste.

serving suggestion
Serve with steamed jasmine rice.

prep + cook time 20 minutes **serves** 4
nutritional count per serving 3.9g total fat (1.1g saturated fat); 727kJ (174 cal); 15.7g carbohydrate; 15.5g protein; 5.3g fibre

creamy mushroom & spinach gnocchi

- 625g (1¼ pounds) fresh potato gnocchi
- 375g (12 ounces) assorted mushrooms, sliced thinly
- 2 cloves garlic, crushed
- 300ml (½ pint) pouring cream
- 90g (3 ounces) baby spinach leaves
- ⅓ cup (25g) finely grated parmesan

1 Cook gnocchi in a large saucepan of boiling water until tender; drain.

2 Cook mushrooms and garlic in a heated oiled large frying pan, over high heat, stirring, 5 minutes or until softened. Add cream and spinach; bring to the boil. Reduce heat to low, simmer, uncovered, until spinach wilts and sauce thickens. Stir in half the parmesan. Season.

3 Add gnocchi to the pan, stir gently to combine. Serve gnocchi topped with remaining parmesan.

serving suggestion
Serve with a rocket salad.

tips Use a variety of mushrooms, such as button, flat, cup and portobello. Or, using just the button variety is fine too. Gnocchi is ready when it floats to the surface of the water.

prep + cook time
10 minutes **serves** 4
nutritional count per serving 36.2g total fat (23.4g saturated fat); 2458kJ (588 cal); 48.2g carbohydrate; 14.4g protein; 6.8g fibre

grilled lamb chops with tomato & olive salsa

- ¼ cup loosely packed fresh oregano leaves
- 8 lamb loin chops (800g)
- 250g (8 ounces) cherry tomatoes, quartered
- ½ cup (75g) seeded kalamata olives, halved
- 2 tablespoons french dressing
- 100g (3 ounces) rocket (arugula)

1 Finely chop half the oregano; combine with chops in a large bowl.

2 Season chops; cook on a heated oiled grill plate (or grill or barbecue) for 4 minutes each side or until cooked as desired.

3 Meanwhile, to make tomato and olive salsa, combine tomato, olives, dressing and remaining oregano in a medium bowl. Season to taste.

4 Serve chops with salsa and rocket.

serving suggestion
Serve with roast potatoes or warm crusty bread.

prep + cook time
10 minutes serves 4
nutritional count per
serving 16.2g total fat
(6.6g saturated fat);
1333kJ (319 cal);
8.2g carbohydrate;
33.9g protein; 2.2g fibre

tips Some butchers sell a pork and veal mixture, however, if it is not available, buy half the amount each of pork and veal mince and combine.

sang choy bow

- 2 teaspoons sesame oil
- 1 medium brown onion (150g), chopped finely
- 2 cloves garlic, crushed
- 600g (1¼ ounces) minced (ground) pork and veal mixture
- ¼ cup (60ml) light soy sauce
- ¼ cup (60ml) oyster sauce
- 1 medium red capsicum (bell pepper) (200g), chopped finely
- 3 cups (240g) bean sprouts
- 4 green onions (scallions), chopped coarsely
- 8 large iceberg lettuce leaves
- 1 tablespoon toasted sesame seeds

1 Heat oil in a wok; stir-fry brown onion and garlic, over medium heat, until onion softens. Add mince; stir-fry until cooked through. Add sauces and capsicum; reduce heat, simmer, uncovered, stirring occasionally, 3 minutes.
2 Just before serving, stir sprouts and green onion into mixture. Divide sang choy bow into lettuce leaves; sprinkle with sesame seeds to serve.

serving suggestion
Add 100g thick rice noodles to the mince and you have a delicious Asian stir-fry.

prep + cook time
25 minutes **serves** 4
nutritional count per serving 14.8g total fat
4.6g saturated fat
1388kJ (331 cal)
10.4g carbohydrate
37.1g protein 3.4g fibre

- 4 firm white fish fillets (800g)
- ⅓ cup (80ml) peri peri marinade
- 120g (4 ounces) mixed salad leaves
- 1 tablespoon lemon juice

1 Drizzle fish with marinade, coating both sides. Cook fish, in batches, in a heated oiled large frying pan, 3 minutes each side or until cooked through.

2 Meanwhile, combine leaves and juice in a medium bowl, season; serve with fish.

serving suggestion Serve with barbecued sweet corn, if you like.

peri peri fish

tip Use a fish such as snapper or perch.

prep + cook time 20 minutes **serves** 4 **nutritional count per serving** 5g total fat (1.5g saturated fat); 978kJ (234 cal); 4.4g carbohydrate; 41.4g protein; 1.6g fibre

prep + cook time
15 minutes **serves** 4
nutritional count per serving 24.5g total fat
(5.3g saturated fat); 2884kJ
(690 cal); 38g carbohydrate;
76.2g protein; 4.8g fibre

tip There are many types of tortillas available, you can use corn or wholemeal tortillas for this recipe.

mexican chicken wraps

- 16 chicken tenderloins (1.2kg)
- 35g (1 ounce) packet taco seasoning mix
- 8 large (26cm/10-inch) flour tortillas
- 1 large avocado (320g), mashed
- 2 cups shredded cos (romaine) lettuce leaves
- 2 large tomatoes (440g), chopped coarsely

1 Toss chicken in seasoning mix. Cook chicken on a heated oiled grill plate (or grill or barbecue), 4 minutes each side or until cooked through.

2 Meanwhile, warm tortillas according to packet directions.

3 Spread tortillas with avocado; top with lettuce, tomato and chicken. Roll wraps to enclose filling.

serving suggestion Serve with sour cream, coriander (cilantro) leaves and lime wedges.

easy main meals

Here are those dishes that most cooks can whip up without looking at a recipe. They are everyone's favourite and not as hard to master as you think. Invite your friends over to share.

tips You need to cook 1 cup (200g) rice for this recipe. Or, use two 250g sachets of pre-cooked jasmine rice. Nasi goreng seasoning is a spice paste found in sachets in the Asian food section of supermarkets.

nasi goreng with pork

- 500g (1 pound) pork strips
- 1 large red capsicum (bell pepper) (350g), chopped coarsely
- 4 green onions (scallions), cut into 3cm (1¼-inch) lengths
- 60g (2-ounce) packet nasi goreng seasoning
- 3 cups (450g) cooked jasmine rice (see tips)
- ½ cup loosely packed fresh coriander (cilantro) leaves

1 Stir-fry pork, in batches, in a heated oiled wok until browned all over. Remove from wok.

2 Add capsicum and onion to wok; stir-fry until just tender. Add nasi goreng seasoning; stir-fry 1 minute. Add rice, pork and coriander; stir-fry until heated through.

serving suggestion
Serve topped with a fried egg.

prep + cook time
15 minutes **serves** 4
**nutritional count per
serving** 10.5g total fat
(3.4g saturated fat);
1672kJ (400 cal);
43.3g carbohydrate;
31.3g protein; 2.6g fibre

tips Use any curry paste you like. To boost the flavour of the soup, choose a hot curry paste, or add some finely chopped fresh chilli.

vegetable &
red lentil soup

- **2 tablespoons curry paste**
- **800g (1½-pounds) canned diced tomatoes**
- **3 cups (750ml) chicken stock**
- **1 medium carrot (120g), chopped finely**
- **2 sticks celery (300g), trimmed, chopped finely**
- **1 medium potato (200g), chopped finely**
- **1 large zucchini (150g), chopped finely**
- **⅔ cup (130g) dried red lentils**
- **½ cup (60g) frozen peas**
- **⅓ cup (95g) low-fat plain yoghurt**
- **⅓ cup coarsely chopped fresh coriander (cilantro) leaves**

1 Cook curry paste in a heated large saucepan, over medium heat, stirring, about one minute or until fragrant. Add tomatoes, stock, carrot, celery, potato and zucchini; bring to the boil. Reduce heat; simmer, covered, 5 minutes.

2 Add lentils to soup mixture; return to the boil. Reduce heat; simmer, uncovered, about 10 minutes or until lentils are just tender. Add peas; return to the boil. Reduce heat; simmer, uncovered, until peas are just tender.

3 Remove soup from heat; stir in yoghurt and coriander leaves.

serving suggestion
Serve with pappadums.

prep + cook time
30 minutes **serves** 4
nutritional count per serving 6.3g total fat (1.5g saturated fat); 1163kJ (278 cal); 34.5g carbohydrate; 14.8g protein; 12.4g fibre

minestrone

- ⅔ cup (130g) dried borlotti beans
- 1 tablespoon olive oil
- 1 small brown onion (80g), chopped coarsely
- 1 clove garlic, crushed
- 2 tablespoons tomato paste
- 1 litre (4 cups) water
- 1½ cups (375ml) vegetable stock
- 700g (1½ pounds) bottled tomato pasta sauce
- 1 trimmed celery stalk (100g), chopped finely
- 1 small carrot (70g), chopped finely
- 1 small zucchini (90g), chopped finely
- 55g (2 ounces) green beans, trimmed, chopped finely
- ½ cup (90g) macaroni
- ¼ cup coarsely chopped fresh basil

1 Place borlotti beans in a medium bowl, cover with water; stand overnight, drain. Rinse under cold water; drain.
2 Heat oil in a large saucepan, over medium heat; cook onion and garlic, stirring, 4 minutes or until onion softens. Add paste; cook, stirring, 2 minutes. Add borlotti beans, the water, stock and pasta sauce; bring to the boil. Reduce heat; simmer, uncovered, about 1 hour or until beans are tender.

3 Add celery to soup; simmer, uncovered, 10 minutes. Add carrot, zucchini and green beans; simmer, uncovered, about 20 minutes or until carrot is tender. Add macaroni; simmer until pasta is tender.
4 Serve soup in bowls sprinkled with basil.
serving suggestion Sprinkle soup with parmesan, serve with warm crusty bread.

tips Minestrone can be made up to 2 days ahead; cover, refrigerate. You can use 400g (12½ ounces) canned borlotti beans instead of dried ones; add them with the green beans.

prep + cook time 2 hours
30 minutes (+ standing)
serves 4
**nutritional count per
serving** 5.5g total fat
(1g saturated fat);
1095kJ (262 cal);
39.9g carbohydrate;
9.4g protein; 6.5g fibre

prep + cook time 6½ hours
serves 6
**nutritional count per
serving** 8.5g total fat
(2.9g saturated fat); 765kJ
(183 cal); 5.8g carbohydrate;
19.9g protein; 2.2g fibre

tips This is a great recipe for entertaining in the cooler months. Lamb shoulder chops and chump chops are also suitable for this recipe.

slow-cooker lamb chops

- **12 lamb forequarter chops (2kg)**
- **2 tablespoons plain (all-purpose) flour**
- **2 tablespoons olive oil**
- **80g (2½ ounces) packaged french onion soup mix**
- **2 medium leeks (700g), sliced thinly**
- **3 stalks celery (450g), trimmed, chopped coarsely**
- **2 cups (500ml) salt-reduced chicken stock**
- **¼ cup coarsely chopped fresh flat-leaf parsley**

1 Trim excess fat from lamb. Toss lamb in flour to coat, shake off excess. Heat oil in a large frying pan; cook lamb, in batches, until browned.

2 Place 4 lamb chops into a 4.5-litre (18-cup) slow cooker. Sprinkle one-third of the soup mix then one-third of the leek and celery over the chops. Repeat layering with remaining lamb, soup mix, leek and celery. Pour stock into cooker. Cook, covered, on low, 6 hours.

3 Remove lamb from cooker; cover to keep warm. Skim fat from surface of sauce; season to taste. Serve lamb and sauce sprinkled with parsley.

serving suggestion Serve with mashed or roast potatoes, and steamed green beans.

lamb rissoles
with rosemary gravy

- **500g (1 pound) minced (ground) lamb**
- **1 large brown onion (200g), grated coarsely**
- **1 clove garlic, crushed**
- **½ cup (35g) fresh breadcrumbs**
- **1 egg**
- **1 tablespoon olive oil**
- **500g (1 pound) baby new potatoes**
- **30g (1 ounce) butter**
- **1 tablespoon plain (all-purpose) flour**
- **1 cup (250ml) beef stock**
- **1 tablespoon fresh rosemary leaves**
- **250g (8 ounces) cherry tomatoes**

1 Combine lamb, onion, garlic, breadcrumbs and egg in a medium bowl. Shape mixture into eight rissoles.

2 Heat oil in a large frying pan over medium heat; cook rissoles, in batches, about 15 minutes or until cooked through. Drain on paper towel; cover with foil to keep warm. Reserve pan with rissole drippings.

3 Meanwhile, boil, steam or microwave potatoes until tender; drain. Crush potatoes in a medium bowl with a potato masher; stir in butter.

4 Cook flour in rissole pan over high heat, stirring, until mixture browns and bubbles. Gradually stir in stock; stir until gravy boils and thickens. Strain gravy; add rosemary.

5 Meanwhile, cook tomatoes, stirring, in a heated small frying pan over medium heat about 2 minutes or until split and just softened.

6 Serve rissoles with potato and tomatoes; top with gravy.

prep + cook time
55 minutes **serves** 4
nutritional count per serving 23.7g total fat
(10.2g saturated fat);
1898kJ (454 cal);
26.4g carbohydrate;
33.7g protein; 3.9 fibre

tip Rissoles can be prepared up to 2 days in advance; cover, refrigerate. Uncooked rissoles can be frozen for up to 3 months.

tips We used fettuccine in this recipe, but you can use the pasta of your choice. The bolognese sauce can be frozen in an airtight container for up to three months.

fettuccine bolognese

- 1 tablespoon olive oil
- 1 large brown onion (200g), chopped finely
- 2 cloves garlic, crushed
- 600g (1¼ pounds) minced (ground) beef
- ¼ cup (70g) tomato paste
- 1 cup (125ml) beef stock
- 800g (1½ pounds) canned diced tomatoes
- ⅓ cup finely chopped fresh flat-leaf parsley
- 1 tablespoon finely chopped fresh oregano
- 375g (12 ounces) fettuccine
- ½ cup (40g) flaked parmesan

1 Heat oil in a large frying pan, over medium heat; cook onion and garlic, stirring, until onion softens.
2 Add beef; cook, stirring, until browned. Add paste, stock and tomatoes; bring to the boil. Reduce heat to low; simmer, covered, 20 minutes. Uncover; simmer about 10 minutes or until thickened slightly. Remove from heat; stir in herbs. Season to taste.

3 Meanwhile, cook fettuccine in a large saucepan of boiling water until tender; drain.
4 Serve fettuccine topped with bolognese and parmesan.
serving suggestion Serve with a leafy green salad and warm crusty bread.

VARIATIONS
chilli con carne Add 1 teaspoon ground cumin and 1 teaspoon dried chilli flakes with beef at step 2. Add 420g (13½ ounce) canned rinsed drained four-bean mix at the end of step 2. Omit steps 3 and 4. Serve with 3 cups steamed rice in place of the fettuccine.

cottage pie Add 2 cups frozen pea, corn and carrot mix to beef for last 5 minutes of step 2. Omit steps 3 and 4. Boil, steam or microwave 800g (1½ pounds) coarsely chopped potatoes until tender; drain. Mash in a medium bowl with 20g (¾ ounce) butter and ½ cup hot milk until smooth. Place beef mixture in a deep 2-litre (8-cup) ovenproof dish; top with mashed potato, sprinkle with ½ cup (60g) coarsely grated cheddar cheese. Grill 10 minutes or until browned lightly.

prep + cook time 1 hour
serves 4
nutritional count per serving 20g total fat (7.4g saturated fat); 2893kJ (692 cal); 75g carbohydrate; 48.4g protein; 7.3g fibre

beef stroganoff

- 2 tablespoons vegetable oil
- 600g (1¼ ounces) beef rump steak, sliced thinly
- 1 medium brown onion (150g), sliced thinly
- 2 cloves garlic, crushed
- 1 teaspoon sweet paprika
- 400g (12½ ounces) button mushrooms, sliced thickly
- 2 tablespoons dry red wine
- 1 tablespoon lemon juice
- 2 tablespoons tomato paste
- 1¼ cups (300g) sour cream
- 1 tablespoon coarsely chopped fresh dill

1 Heat half the oil in a large frying pan over high heat; cook beef, in batches, until browned lightly. Remove from pan.

2 Heat remaining oil in the same pan; cook onion and garlic, stirring, 4 minutes or until onion softens. Add paprika and mushrooms; cook, stirring, 3 minutes or until mushrooms are tender, season to taste.

3 Return beef to pan with wine and juice; bring to the boil. Reduce heat; simmer, covered, about 5 minutes or until beef is tender. Add paste, sour cream and dill; cook, stirring, until heated through. Serve stroganoff with steamed rice.

serving suggestion
As an alternative to rice, serve stroganoff with mashed potato or fettuccine.

tip Sweet paprika, also known as hungarian paprika, is a spice derived from various forms of dried capsicum (bell pepper), and is used extensively throughout Europe. It's one of the defining flavours of a stroganoff. Don't be tempted to use smoked paprika (used in Spanish cooking), it will overwhelm the flavours of the dish.

prep + cook time
35 minutes **serves** 4
**nutritional count per
serving** 43.3g total fat
(22.4g saturated fat);
2462kJ (589 cal);
5.9g carbohydrate;
41.4g protein; 3.7g fibre

tips Macaroni takes about 12 minutes to cook to al dente. Recipe can be prepared the day before, cover, refrigerate. Remove from refrigerator 30 minutes prior to baking.

macaroni cheese

- 300g (9½ ounces) macaroni
- 4 rindless bacon rashers (260g), chopped finely
- 50g (1½ ounces) butter
- ⅓ cup (50g) plain (all-purpose) flour
- 1 litre (4 cups) milk
- 1 cup (120g) coarsely grated cheddar cheese
- ½ cup (40g) finely grated pecorino cheese
- 2 tablespoons wholegrain mustard
- ½ cup (35g) stale breadcrumbs
- 20g (¾ ounce) butter, extra

1 Preheat oven to 180°C/350°F. Oil a deep 2-litre (8-cup) ovenproof dish.

2 Cook pasta in a large saucepan of boiling water until tender; drain.

3 Meanwhile, cook bacon in a medium saucepan, over high heat, stirring, until crisp; drain on paper towel.

4 Melt butter in the same pan, over medium heat, add flour; cook, stirring, 1 minute. Gradually stir in milk; cook, stirring, until sauce boils and thickens. Cool 2 minutes; stir in cheeses and mustard.

5 Combine pasta, sauce and bacon in a large bowl; season to taste. Pour mixture into ovenproof dish. Top with breadcrumbs, dot with extra butter. Bake, about 30 minutes or until browned.

serving suggestion Serve with a leafy green salad.

prep + cook time 1 hour
serves 4
nutritional count per serving 47.5g total fat (27.8g saturated fat); 3854kJ (922 cal); 78.8g carbohydrate; 43.1g protein; 3.5g fibre

tip Ask the butcher to roll and tie the pork at 2cm (¾-inch) intervals for you, and to score the rind, if it isn't already done.

roast loin of pork

- **2 sprigs rosemary**
- **2.5kg (5-pound) boneless loin of pork, rind on, rolled and tied at 2cm (¾-inch) intervals**
- **1 tablespoon olive oil**
- **1 tablespoon coarse cooking (kosher) salt**

prep + cook time 2 hours (+ standing) **serves** 8
nutritional count per serving 29.2g total fat (10.6g saturated fat); 2161kJ (517 cal); 0g carbohydrate; 64.1g protein; 0g fibre

1 Preheat oven to 250°C/485°F.
2 Tuck the rosemary under the string around the pork. Place pork in a large baking dish; rub rind with oil then salt. Roast about 40 minutes or until rind blisters. Drain excess fat from dish.
3 Reduce oven to 180°C/350°F. Roast pork about 1 hour.
4 Transfer pork to a plate; cover, stand 15 minutes before carving.

serving suggestions
Serve pork with roasted vegetables and apple sauce. Buy ready-made apple sauce from the supermarket or try making your own by cooking coarsely chopped, peeled apples with a little water in a small saucepan, about 10 minutes or until apple is soft. Stir in sugar and ground cinnamon to taste.

tips Tucking the wings under the body prevents them from burning and drying out during cooking. Rubbing the butter mixture over the chicken will give you that beautiful crisp skin on the chicken.

roast chicken
with tomato & beans

- 2kg (4 pound) chicken
- 1 medium lemon (140g), quartered
- 6 sprigs fresh thyme
- 6 cloves garlic, unpeeled
- 60g (2 ounces) butter, softened
- 2 tablespoons lemon juice
- 2 cloves garlic, crushed
- 2 teaspoons finely chopped fresh thyme
- 1 cup (250ml) water
- 1 tablespoon olive oil
- 1 medium brown onion (150g), chopped coarsely
- 1kg (2 pounds) green beans, trimmed
- 4 medium tomatoes (600g), chopped coarsely

prep + cook time
2 hours 40 minutes
serves 6
nutritional count per serving 33.5g total fat
(12.7g saturated fat); 2123kJ
(508 cal); 8.3g carbohydrate;
40.3g protein; 7.3g fibre

1 Preheat oven to 200°C/400°F.
2 Wash and pat dry chicken with paper towel. Tuck wing tips under chicken. Fill cavity with lemon, thyme sprigs and garlic, fold skin over to enclose filling; secure with toothpicks. Tie legs together with kitchen string.
3 Combine butter, juice, crushed garlic and chopped thyme in a small bowl; season. Rub butter mixture all over chicken.
4 Place chicken on an oiled rack in a large baking dish; pour the water into dish. Roast about 2 hours, basting occasionally with pan juices.

5 Meanwhile, heat oil in a large saucepan, over medium heat; cook onion, stirring, 4 minutes or until onion softens. Add beans and tomato; cook, over low heat, covered, stirring occasionally, about 20 minutes or until vegetables soften slightly.
6 Serve chicken with tomato and beans.
serving suggestion
Roast some potatoes with the chicken for the last hour of its cooking time. Simply halve them, spray with cooking oil and place around the chicken on the wire rack.

chicken & leek pie

- **2 cups (500ml) chicken stock**
- **600g (1¼ pounds) chicken breast fillets**
- **1 tablespoon olive oil**
- **40g (1½ ounces) butter**
- **1 large leek (500g), sliced thinly**
- **2 stalks celery (300g), trimmed, chopped finely**
- **2 tablespoons plain (all-purpose) flour**
- **2 teaspoons fresh thyme leaves**
- **½ cup (125ml) milk**
- **1 cup (250ml) pouring cream**
- **2 teaspoons wholegrain mustard**
- **2 sheets ready-rolled shortcrust pastry**
- **1 sheet ready-rolled puff pastry**
- **1 egg yolk**

prep + cook time
1 hour 35 minutes
serves 6
nutritional count
per serving 56g total fat
(30.1g saturated fat); 3344kJ
(800 cal); 42.5g carbohydrate;
31.1g protein; 3.6g fibre

1 Bring stock to the boil in a medium saucepan. Add chicken; return to the boil. Reduce heat; simmer, covered, about 10 minutes or until chicken is cooked. Remove from heat; stand chicken in poaching liquid 10 minutes. Remove chicken; chop coarsely. Reserve ⅓ cup (80ml) of the poaching liquid; keep remainder for another use, or discard.

2 Heat oil and butter in a medium saucepan over medium heat; cook leek and celery, stirring, 5 minutes or until leek softens. Add flour and thyme; cook, stirring, 1 minute. Gradually stir in reserved poaching liquid, milk and cream; cook, stirring, until mixture boils and thickens. Stir in chicken and mustard. Cool 10 minutes. Season to taste.

3 Preheat oven to 200°C/400°F. Oil a 1.5-litre (6-cup) ovenproof dish.
4 Line base and side of dish with shortcrust pastry, trim to fit; prick well all over with fork. Bake 10 minutes. Cool 5 minutes. Spoon chicken mixture into pastry case; place puff pastry over filling, trim to fit dish. Brush pastry with egg yolk; cut two small slits in top of pastry. Bake about 20 minutes or until browned lightly.

serving suggestions
Serve with oven-baked chips, peas and corn.

tips Filling can be made a day ahead; cover, refrigerate. You can brush the pastry with a little milk instead of egg, if you like.

tip Use any short pasta –
penne, spirals, shells or bow ties.

pea & salmon bake

- 375g (12 ounces) rigatoni pasta
- 30g (1 ounce) butter
- 2 tablespoons plain (all-purpose) flour
- 2 cups (500ml) milk
- 1½ cups (180g) frozen peas
- ½ cup (40g) coarsely grated parmesan
- 1¼ cups (150g) coarsely grated cheddar cheese
- 415g (13 ounces) canned pink salmon, drained, skin and bones removed

1 Preheat oven to 200°C/400°F.

2 Cook pasta in a large saucepan of boiling water until tender; drain.

3 Meanwhile, melt butter in a medium saucepan over medium heat. Add flour; cook, stirring, until mixture thickens and bubbles. Gradually stir in milk; stir over medium heat until sauce boils and thickens. Stir in peas, ¼ cup parmesan and ¾ cup cheddar.

4 Combine sauce mixture with pasta and salmon in an oiled shallow 2.5-litre (10-cup) ovenproof dish; sprinkle with remaining combined cheeses. Bake, uncovered, about 20 minutes or until browned lightly.

serving suggestion
Serve with salad.

prep + cook time
50 minutes **serves** 6
nutritional count per serving 23.8g total fat
(13.7g saturated fat);
2345kJ (561 cal);
51.2g carbohydrate;
33.1g protein; 3.9g fibre

honey mustard

Whisk together ½ cup mayonnaise, ¼ cup cider vinegar, 1 tablespoon honey and 2 teaspoons wholegrain mustard in a small jug until combined.

tip This classic salad dressing is creamy and sweet with a sharp tang from the cider vinegar.

lemon macadamia

Whisk together 1 teaspoon finely grated lemon rind, ¼ cup lemon juice, ½ cup macadamia oil, ⅓ cup finely chopped roasted macadamia nuts and 1 teaspoon caster (superfine) sugar in small jug until combined.

serving suggestions Serve with seafood salads, or other delicate salads that shouldn't be overpowered by olive oil.

tip Macadamia oil has a mild, unobtrusive nutty flavour.

prep time 5 minutes **makes** 1 cup
nutritional count per tablespoon
4.1g total fat (0.5g saturated fat);
230kJ (55 cal); 4.5g carbohydrate;
0.2g protein; 0.1g fibre

prep time 10 minutes **makes** 1 cup
nutritional count per tablespoon
12.4g total fat (1.8g saturated fat);
477kJ (114 cal); 0.6g carbohydrate;
0.3g protein; 0.2g fibre

dressings

asian lime

Blend 1 tablespoon coarsely chopped fresh
coriander (cilantro) root and stem, 5 cloves
coarsely chopped garlic, 1 teaspoon
black peppercorns, ½ cup lime juice,
1 tablespoon each fish sauce and grated
palm sugar and 2 x 10cm (4-inch) sticks
coarsely chopped fresh lemon grass until
chopped finely. Season to taste.

serving suggestions Serve with seafood,
chicken, beef, lamb or pork. Dressing is
great for Asian-style salads.

sesame soy

Place 1 teaspoon sesame oil, ¼ cup soy
sauce, 1 tablespoon sweet chilli sauce and
2 tablespoons lime juice in a screw-top jar;
shake well. Season to taste.

serving suggestion Serve with chicken or
an Asian noodle salad.

---

prep time 10 minutes **makes** ¾ cup
nutritional count per tablespoon
0g total fat (0g saturated fat);
75kJ (18 cal); 3.3g carbohydrate;
0.5g protein; 0.4g fibre

prep time 5 minutes **makes** ½ cup
nutritional count per tablespoon
0.8g total fat (0.1g saturated fat);
79kJ (19 cal); 2g carbohydrate;
0.6g protein; 0g fibre

peas & mint butter

Boil, steam or microwave 2¼ cups fresh shelled peas until just tender; drain. Meanwhile, combine 40g (1½ ounce) softened butter, 1 tablespoon finely chopped fresh mint and 1 teaspoon finely grated lemon rind in a small bowl. Serve peas topped with butter mixture.
serving suggestion Serve with roast pork or chicken.

tip You can use frozen peas in this recipe if you prefer.

prep + cook time 10 minutes serves 4
nutritional count per serving 8.6g total fat
(5.4g saturated fat); 589kJ (141 cal);
8.6g carbohydrate; 5.2g protein; 5g fibre

broccolini & honey

Halve 700g (1½ pounds) broccolini, crossways. Cook broccolini in a large baking-paper-lined steamer, over a large saucepan of simmering water, about 5 minutes or until tender. Meanwhile, combine 1 tablespoon light soy sauce, 2 teaspoons honey and 1 tablespoon boiling water in small jug. Serve broccolini drizzled with sauce; sprinkle with 2 teaspoons toasted sesame seeds.
serving suggestion Serve with chicken & leek pie (see page 64).

prep + cook time 10 minutes serves 4
nutritional count per serving 1.3g total fat
(0g saturated fat); 326kJ (78 cal);
4.1g carbohydrate; 8.8g protein; 7.3g fibre

kumara mash

Coarsely chop 500g (1 pound) kumara (orange sweet potato) and 500g (1 pound) potatoes; boil, steam or microwave together, until tender; drain. Mash in a large bowl; stir in ¼ cup hot chicken stock and 40g (1½ ounces) melted butter. Season to taste.

serving suggestion Serve with roast pork or chicken.

mashed potato

Boil, steam or microwave 1kg (2 pounds) coarsely chopped potatoes until tender; drain. Using the back of a wooden spoon, push potato through fine sieve into large bowl. Stir in 40g (1½ ounce) butter and ¾ cup hot milk.

serving suggestion Serve with beef stroganoff (see page 56).

tip The trick to getting smooth, creamy mash is to use hot milk instead of cold.

prep + cook time 30 minutes serves 4
nutritional count per serving 8.5g total fat
(5.4g saturated fat); 1024kJ (245 cal);
34.2g carbohydrate; 5.6g protein; 4.3g fibre

prep + cook time 30 minutes serves 4
nutritional count per serving 10.2g total fat
(6.6g saturated fat); 1028kJ (246 cal);
30.1g carbohydrate; 6.7g protein; 3.4g fibre

lemon crush

Stir ⅔ cup lemon butter and ⅓ cup pouring cream in a small saucepan, over low heat, until smooth; cool 10 minutes. Divide and layer 1 litre (4 cups) vanilla ice-cream, lemon butter mixture and 4 crumbled mini pavlova shells in four serving glasses; serve immediately.

tip If you cannot find mini pavlova shells you could use part of a whole meringue shell or coconut macaroons.

rhubarb ice-cream

Line a 14cm x 21cm (5½-inch x 8½-inch) loaf pan with plastic wrap. Cook 2 cups chopped rhubarb and 2 tablespoons brown sugar in a large saucepan, covered, 5 minutes or until rhubarb is almost tender. Simmer, uncovered, 5 minutes or until rhubarb softens but retains its shape. Cool mixture. Place 2 litres (8 cups) softened vanilla ice-cream in a large bowl. Gently swirl in 125g (4 ounces) coarsely chopped Ginger Nut biscuits and rhubarb mixture. Pour ice-cream mixture into pan. Cover; freeze 3 hours or until firm.

prep + cook time 15 minutes
serves 4
nutritional count per serving 23.5g total fat (14.5g saturated fat); 2048kJ (490 cal); 67.3g carbohydrate; 5.4g protein; 0.1g fibre

prep + cook time 20 minutes (+ freezing)
serves 8
nutritional count per serving 17.4g total fat (11.5g saturated fat); 1538kJ (367 cal); 46.8g carbohydrates; 6.7g protein; 0.7g fibre

berry ice-cream sandwich

Fold 2 cups thawed drained frozen
blackberries into 500ml (2 cups) softened
vanilla ice-cream. Working quickly, place
6 Butternut Snap biscuits on a baking-
paper-lined tray; place a scoop of ice-cream
on top of each biscuit, then top with another
6 Butternut Snap biscuits. Press down
gently. Freeze 20 minutes before serving.

turkish delight sundae

Blend or process 150g (4½ ounces)
raspberries until smooth. Divide and layer
1 litre (4 cups) vanilla ice-cream, raspberry
puree, 55g (2 ounces) coarsely chopped
chocolate-coated turkish delight and ½ cup
coarsely chopped roasted pistachios in
six serving glasses. Serve immediately.

tip Turkish delight is a popular Middle-
Eastern sweet.

---

prep time 35 minutes (+ freezing)
serves 4
nutritional count per serving 14.7g total fat
(9.4g saturated fat); 1291kJ (308 cal);
36.7g carbohydrate; 5.2g protein; 6.2g fibre

---

prep time 10 minutes
serves 6
nutritional count per serving 15.4g total fat
(7g saturated fat); 1145kJ (274 cal);
27.1g carbohydrate; 5.9g protein; 2.5g fibre

BAMBOO SHOOTS the tender shoots of bamboo plants, available in cans; must be rinsed and drained before use.

BARLEY a nutritious grain used in soups and stews. Hulled barley, the least processed, is high in fibre. Pearl barley has had the husk removed then been steamed and polished so that only the "pearl" of the original grain remains, much the same as white rice.

BEANS

cannellini a small white bean similar in appearance and flavour to other white beans (great northern, navy or haricot), all of which can be substituted for the other. Available dried or canned.

green also known as french or string beans (although the tough string they once had has generally been bred out of them), this long thin fresh bean is consumed in its entirety once cooked.

lima also known as butter beans; large, flat, kidney-shaped bean, off-white in colour, with a mealy texture and mild taste.

white a generic term we use for canned or dried cannellini, haricot, great northern or navy beans belonging to the same family, *phaseolus vulgaris*.

BEETROOT (BEETS) also known as red beets; firm, round root vegetable.

BROCCOLINI a cross between broccoli and chinese kale; has long asparagus-like stems with a long loose floret, both completely edible. Resembles broccoli but is milder and sweeter in taste.

BUK CHOY also known as bok choy, pak choi, chinese white cabbage or chinese chard; has a fresh, mild mustard taste. Use both stems and leaves. Baby buk choy, also known as *pak kat farang* or shanghai bok choy, is smaller and more tender than buk choy.

BUTTER use salted or unsalted (sweet) butter; 125g is equal to one stick of butter (4 ounces).

CAPERS grey-green buds of a warm climate shrub (usually Mediterranean); sold dried and salted or pickled in a vinegar brine. Rinse before using.

CAPSICUM (BELL PEPPER) Comes in many colours: red, green, yellow, orange and purplish-black. Be sure to discard seeds and membranes before use.

CHEESE

fetta Greek in origin; a crumbly textured goat's- or sheep's-milk cheese with a sharp, salty taste. Ripened and stored in salted whey.

goat's made from goat's milk, has an earthy, strong taste; available in both soft and firm textures, in various shapes and sizes, and sometimes rolled in ash or herbs.

parmesan also called parmigiano; is a hard, grainy cow's-milk cheese originating in Italy. Reggiano is the best variety.

CHICKPEAS (GARBANZO BEANS) also called hummus or channa; an irregularly round, sandy-coloured legume. Has a firm texture even after cooking, a floury mouth-feel and robust nutty flavour; available canned or dried (reconstitute for several hours in cold water before use).

CHILLI generally, the smaller the chilli, the hotter it is. Use rubber gloves when seeding and chopping fresh chillies as they can burn your skin. Removing seeds and membranes lessens the heat level.

long available both fresh and dried; a generic term used for any moderately hot, thin, long (6cm/2¼-inch) chilli.

red thai a small, hot, bright red coloured chilli.

CIABATTA in Italian, the word means slipper, which refers to the traditional shape of this popular crusty, open-textured white sourdough bread.

CINNAMON available in pieces (called sticks or quills) and ground into powder; one of the world's most common spices, used as a sweet, fragrant flavouring for both sweet and savoury foods.

COCONUT

milk not the liquid found inside the fruit (coconut water), but the diluted liquid from the second pressing of the white flesh of a mature coconut.

glossary

CORIANDER (CILANTRO)
also known as pak chee or
chinese parsley; a bright-
green leafy herb with a
pungent flavour. Both the
stems and roots of coriander
are also used in cooking;
wash well before using.
Also available ground or
as seeds; these should not
be substituted for fresh
coriander as the tastes are
completely different.

CREAM

pouring also known as pure
or fresh cream. It has no
additives and contains a
minimum fat content of 35%.

thickened (heavy) a whipping
cream that contains a
thickener. It has a minimum
fat content of 35%.

CUMIN also known as zeera
or comino; has a spicy,
nutty flavour.

CURRY LEAVES available fresh
or dried and have a mild curry
flavour; use like bay leaves.

CURRY PASTES commercially
made pastes vary in strengths
and flavours. Use whichever
one you feel best suits your
spice-level tolerance.

green the hottest of the
traditional pastes; contains
chilli, garlic, onion, salt, lemon
grass, spices and galangal.

red a popular curry paste;
a hot blend of red chilli,
garlic, shallot, lemon grass,
salt, galangal, shrimp paste,
kaffir lime peel, coriander,
cumin and paprika. It is milder
than the hotter thai green
curry paste.

EGGPLANT also known as
aubergine. Ranging in size
from tiny to very large and in
colour from pale green to
deep purple. Can also be
purchased char-grilled,
packed in oil, in jars.

FENNEL also called finocchio
or anise; a white to very pale
green-white, firm, crisp,
roundish vegetable about
8-12cm in diameter. The bulb
has a slightly sweet, anise
flavour but the leaves have a
much stronger taste. Also the
name given to dried seeds
that have a licorice flavour.

FLOUR

plain (all-purpose) an
all-purpose wheat flour.

self-raising plain flour sifted
with baking powder in the
proportion of 1 cup flour to
2 teaspoons baking powder.

GAI LAN also known as
chinese broccoli, gai larn,
kanah, gai lum and chinese
kale; appreciated more for its
stems than its coarse leaves.

GARAM MASALA a blend
of spices that includes
cardamom, cinnamon,
coriander, cloves, fennel and
cumin. Black pepper and chilli
can be added for heat.

GOW GEE WRAPPERS also
called wonton wrappers or
spring roll pastry sheets, are
found in the refrigerated or
freezer section of Asian food
shops and many supermarkets.
These come in different
thicknesses and shapes. Thin
wrappers work best in soups,
while the thicker ones are

best for frying; and the
choice of round or square,
small or large is dependent
on the recipe.

KAFFIR LIME LEAVES also
known as bai magrood.
Aromatic leaves of a citrus
tree; two glossy dark
green leaves joined end to
end, forming a rounded
hourglass shape. A strip of
fresh lime peel may be
substituted for each kaffir
lime leaf.

KECAP MANIS a thick soy
sauce with added sugar and
spices. The sweetness is
derived from the addition
of molasses or palm sugar.

**KUMARA (ORANGE
SWEET POTATO)** the
Polynesian name of an
orange-fleshed sweet potato
often confused with yam.

LEEK a member of the
onion family, the leek
resembles a green onion but
is much larger and more
subtle in flavour. Tender
baby or pencil leeks can be
eaten whole with minimal
cooking but adult leeks are
usually trimmed of most of
the green tops then chopped
or sliced.

LEMON GRASS a tall, clumping,
lemon-smelling and -tasting,
sharp-edged grass; only the
white lower part of the stem
is used, finely chopped,
in cooking.

LENTILS (red, brown, yellow)
dried pulses often identified
by and named after their
colour; also known as dhal.

ONIONS

green (scallions) also known incorrectly, as shallots; an immature onion picked before the bulb has formed. Has a long, bright-green edible stalk.

shallots also called french shallots, golden shallots or eschalots; small, brown-skinned, elongated members of the onion family.

spring have small white bulbs and long, narrow, green-leafed tops.

POLENTA also known as cornmeal; a flour-like cereal made of ground corn (maize). Also the name of the dish made from it.

QUINOA pronounced keen-wa; is a gluten-free grain. It has a delicate, slightly nutty taste and chewy texture.

RISONI small rice-shape pasta; very similar to another small pasta, orzo.

SAFFRON available ground or in strands; imparts a yellow-orange colour to food once infused. The quality can vary greatly; the best is the most expensive spice in the world.

SAMBAL OELEK (also ulek or olek) Indonesian in origin; a salty paste made from ground chillies and vinegar. Found in supermarkets and Asian food stores.

SILVER BEET also known as swiss chard; mistakenly called spinach.

SNOW PEAS also called mange tout (eat all). *Snow pea tendrils*, the growing shoots of the plant, are also available at greengrocers.

snow pea sprouts are the tender new growths of snow peas.

SOY SAUCE made from fermented soya beans. Several variations are available in most supermarkets and Asian food stores. We use japanese soy sauce unless otherwise indicated.

SPINACH also known as english spinach and, incorrectly, silver beet.

SUGAR, BROWN very soft, finely granulated sugar retaining molasses for its characteristic colour and flavour.

SUMAC a purple-red, astringent spice ground from berries growing on shrubs that flourish wild around the mediterranean; adds a tart, lemony flavour to food. Available from spice shops and major supermarkets.

TAHINI a rich, sesame-seed paste, used in most Middle-Eastern cuisines, especially Lebanese, in dips and sauces.

TOMATO

bottled pasta sauce a prepared sauce; a blend of tomatoes, herbs and spices.

canned whole peeled tomatoes in natural juices; available crushed, chopped or diced. Use undrained.

paste triple-concentrated tomato puree used to flavour soups, stews and sauces.

puree canned pureed tomatoes (not tomato paste).

TAMARIND found in Asian food shops. Gives a sweet-sour, slightly astringent taste to marinades, pastes, sauces and dressings.

TAMARIND CONCENTRATE (or paste) the commercial result of the distillation of tamarind juice into a condensed, compacted paste.

TRUSS small vine-ripened tomatoes with vine still attached.

TURMERIC also called kamin; is a rhizome related to galangal and ginger. Must be grated or pounded to release its acrid aroma and pungent flavour. Known for the golden colour it imparts, fresh turmeric can be substituted with the more commonly found dried powder.

WATERCRESS one of the cress family, a large group of peppery greens. Highly perishable, so must be used as soon as possible.

YOGHURT, GREEK-STYLE plain yoghurt strained in a cloth (traditionally muslin) to remove the whey and to give it a creamy consistency.

ZA'ATAR a Middle Eastern herb and spice mixture which varies; always includes thyme, with ground sumac and, usually, toasted sesame seeds.

ZUCCHINI also called courgette; small, pale-green, dark-green or yellow vegetable of the squash family.

conversion chart

measures

One Australian metric measuring cup holds approximately 250ml, one Australian metric tablespoon holds 20ml, one Australian metric teaspoon holds 5ml. The difference between one country's measuring cups and another's is within a 2- or 3-teaspoon variance, and will not affect your cooking results. North America, New Zealand and the United Kingdom use a 15ml tablespoon. All cup and spoon measurements are level. The most accurate way of measuring dry ingredients is to weigh them. When measuring liquids, use a clear glass or plastic jug with metric markings. We use large eggs with an average weight of 60g.

dry measures

METRIC	IMPERIAL
15g	½oz
30g	1oz
60g	2oz
90g	3oz
125g	4oz (¼lb)
155g	5oz
185g	6oz
220g	7oz
250g	8oz (½lb)
280g	9oz
315g	10oz
345g	11oz
375g	12oz (¾lb)
410g	13oz
440g	14oz
470g	15oz
500g	16oz (1lb)
750g	24oz (1½lb)
1kg	32oz (2lb)

liquid measures

METRIC	IMPERIAL
30ml	1 fluid oz
60ml	2 fluid oz
100ml	3 fluid oz
125ml	4 fluid oz
150ml	5 fluid oz
190ml	6 fluid oz
250ml	8 fluid oz
300ml	10 fluid oz
500ml	16 fluid oz
600ml	20 fluid oz
1000ml (1 litre)	1¾ pints

length measures

METRIC	IMPERIAL
3mm	⅛in
6mm	¼in
1cm	½in
2cm	¾in
2.5cm	1in
5cm	2in
6cm	2½in
8cm	3in
10cm	4in
13cm	5in
15cm	6in
18cm	7in
20cm	8in
23cm	9in
25cm	10in
28cm	11in
30cm	12in (1ft)

oven temperatures

These oven temperatures are only a guide for conventional ovens. For fan-forced ovens, check the manufacturer's manual.

	°C (CELSIUS)	°F (FAHRENHEIT)
Very slow	120	250
Slow	150	275-300
Moderately slow	160	325
Moderate	180	350-375
Moderately hot	200	400
Hot	220	425-450
Very hot	240	475

The imperial measurements used in these recipes are approximate only. Measurements for cake pans are approximate only. Using same-shaped cake pans of a similar size should not affect the outcome of your baking. We measure the inside top of the cake pan to determine sizes.

index

Published in 2013 by Bauer Media Books, Sydney

Bauer Media Books are published by Bauer Media Limited

54 Park St, Sydney

GPO Box 4088, Sydney, NSW 2001.

phone (02) 9282 8618; fax (02) 9126 3702

www.awwcookbooks.com.au

MEDIA GROUP

BAUER MEDIA BOOKS

Publishing Director - Gerry Reynolds

Publisher - Sally Wright

Editorial & Food Director - Pamela Clark

Director of Sales, Marketing & Rights - Brian Cearnes

Creative Director - Hieu Chi Nguyen

Food Concept Director - Sophia Young

Published and Distributed in the United Kingdom by Octopus Publishing Group

Endeavour House

189 Shaftesbury Avenue

London WC2H 8JY

United Kingdom

phone (+44)(0)207 632 5400; fax (+44)(0)207 632 5405

info@octopus-publishing.co.uk;

www.octopusbooks.co.uk

Printed by 1010 Printing, China

International foreign language rights, Brian Cearnes, Bauer Media Books

bcearnes@bauer-media.com.au

A catalogue record for this book is available from the British Library.

ISBN 9781907428869

© Bauer Media Limited 2013

ABN 18 053 273 546